COSY

The British Art of Comfort

Laura Weir

Illustrations by Rose Electra Harris

yellow
kite

ABOUT THE AUTHOR

Credited by the *New York Times* as a 'Londoner to know', Laura Weir is the editor-in-chief of London *Evening Standard*'s weekly, *ES magazine*. She also writes a weekly column for the newspaper, her topics include London life, raising a young child, and never wanting to miss out on anything that life has to offer. She has written for a huge range of national and international titles, and formerly held senior roles at *British Vogue* and *The Sunday Times*. Laura is on the British Fashion Council's Press Committee and is the co-founder of wearemoody.com, an online platform dedicated to women's mental health and wellbeing.

© Gabrielle Cooper

*This book is dedicated to my mum,
my best friend and a hug of a woman.*

First published in Great Britain in 2018 by Yellow Kite
An imprint of Hodder & Stoughton
An Hachette UK company

1

A CIP catalogue record for this title is available from the British Library

Hardback ISBN 978 1 473 69622 8
eBook ISBN 978 1 473 69623 5

Typeset in Plantin Light by Hewer Text UK Ltd, Edinburgh
Printed and bound in Great Britain by Clays Ltd, Elcograf S.p.A.

Hodder & Stoughton policy is to use papers that are natural, renewable
and recyclable products and made from wood grown in sustainable
forests. The logging and manufacturing processes are expected to
conform to the environmental regulations of the country of origin.

Yellow Kite
Hodder & Stoughton Ltd
Carmelite House
50 Victoria Embankment
London EC4Y 0DZ

www.yellowkitebooks.co.uk
www.hodder.co.uk

CONTENTS

A NOTE ON COSINESS

By Dolly Alderton,
writer and journalist

'Cosiness was something I always slightly feared. Cosiness would mean not being out - and Out was where, I had been lead to believe, life happens. Being out was glamorous, sexy, full of experiences and people. It was rock 'n' roll. It was where you were supposed to be if you wanted to make the most out of your "one wild and precious life", in the words of Mary Oliver. As I've grown up, I've come to realise that so many experiences, lessons and moments of life-changing joy, love and happiness happen in a home. Cosiness, for me, is Radio 4, slow-cooking, every Sunday supplement, long breakfasts, long movies, long phone calls, big jumpers, tangled limbs in a bed or sofa. I enjoy those things even more now that I know indulging them doesn't mean I'm missing out on the big party of life happening somewhere outside and that life can be just as wild and precious in the quiet as it is in the noise.'

INTRODUCTION

I can remember the precise moment that I first identified a cosy feeling. It was the unusually cold winter of 1990 and I'd been sledging with my dad in Greenwich Park, in South East London. We came home, wet, frozen and rosy-cheeked, and sat in front of our log fire with a bowl of Heinz tomato soup, dipping (slightly stale) brown bread that had been coated with margarine into its smooth, scarlet loveliness. The soup was steaming, the fire was crackling and I was slowly thawing. That was cosy. And the soup wasn't the only important ingredient – I was with my parents, and that reassuring comfort of being with people you love is key. There was also the log fire, of course; it's an alchemic thing – we all know a storage heater just doesn't kick out the same cosy vibe as crackling logs, despite them being petrol-station-bought, rather than forest-felled. I had been out in the wind and snow and had retreated to warm up. That's cosy too.

Years later, and I feel like retreating again. But this time it's not from something as natural and as fleeting as the weather. I work in newspapers and live in London. In my daily life, I am surrounded by noise and opinion, and over the past few years I have found myself seeking comfort from politically dark winters and the relentlessly bleak news cycle. My instinct has evolved and become an undeniable urge to hide away and find solitude. Rather than swipe and scroll my way through life, I want to feel protected and nurtured. I don't just want to drink a warm cup of tea, I want my emotional state to mirror that of a cuppa too – warm, predictable, reassuring.

Perhaps I'm just getting old, but I want to swap toxic politics and the anxieties induced by social media for reliability and kindness. I want to feel more cosy.

So this is a hug of a book, conceived to share a few tools to soften the edges of life. It is a paean to retreating; a manual, a text that gives us all permission to seek solace and comfort in harsh times. Being cosy is the antidote to what sometimes feels like a brittle, cold world. It is a theme and a way of life that is universal, and one that people are seeking out more than ever (the hashtag #cosy has 4.4 million results on Instagram, while #cozy has 7.3 million).

The phenomenon of hygge and its concept of homeliness and tucking ourselves in has already piqued our interest, and although it promotes a beautiful cultural lifestyle, there is a certain elitism attached to it now it's been hijacked by hipsters and interior design magazines. The British anthropologist Richard Jenkins has described hygge as 'normative to the point of being close to coercive', and the aggressive way it has been marketed has diluted the pleasantness, and its true meaning.

Whereas cosy . . . Well, cosy is the thing you do when no one is watching. It's not an image or a way of life, it's knitted into the fabric of our wonderful, diverse, eclectic, eccentric British society, through basic, quotidian pleasures such as tea and socks and fires. Cosy is *your* interpretation of what cosy is. Your version will be different from mine, but one thing is for sure: fairy lights don't have to be involved unless you want them to be. In the British Isles, being cold gives us permission to be lazy, and there is nothing better than that. Stopping still and cosying up has become the greatest luxury of our time.

TEA

TEA

'Would you like an adventure now, or should we have our tea first?'

Alice in Wonderland

Life-affirming and soul-warming, a cup of tea solves everything. Your wife has left you? Have a nice cup of tea. The boiler's broken? Put the kettle on. Trump has declared war? Mine's an Earl Grey. Drinking tea is a ritual upon which most of us rely: we boil the water and drown the bag, stirring in a spoonful of comfort as we go. A cuppa kick-starts our day and mends our broken hearts. It's soothing and today, it's a reasonably affordable staple. There's Assam, Ceylon, green and gunpowder, loose-leaf Lapsang and PG tips, there's Yorkshire and Tetley's; made with a mountain of sugar for builders and left black for the more purist among you. There's a herbal tea for every symptom and desired feeling; detox, love or night time tea. There are the colleagues you make tea for, marking a well-earned pause in the day. Whether it's taken in an enormous Sports Direct mug (isn't it amazing that tea is 'taken' – are there any other drinks that have risen to such status?), or in the finest Wedgwood china, a cup of tea gives us all the opportunity to down tools and take a break.

There are mindful moments to be stolen in tea, as you watch the spoon stirring up whirlpools: drifting off into dreamland in the cold light of morning. On the face of it, tea is one of life's everyday indulgences, but that's not all. It's divisive and wonderful and there's a romance to the courtship of a cuppa. 'How do you take yours?' seems an unobtrusive question, yet the answer it elicits tells you so much about a person. If she asks for an alternative milk: 'I bet she's hard work'. More than one sugar: 'Doesn't he read the news?'. Some may call it snobbery, I like to think of it as a social study, an enquiry laden with loving judgement. And then there's the question of what to drink it in. Back to that Sports Direct mug or the finest bone china? You can buy tea sets for one – a mug and pot that stack, one upon the other – which puts paid to the saying that it is in fact for two. Tea drinking can, however, be a glorious solo pursuit, especially on a hangover and accompanied by a packet of Hobnobs and a Netflix account.

Tea isn't frisky or fun, it's a tender, bosomy wet snog. You don't take someone upstairs for a tea – it's not saucy like coffee. Tea is restorative and nurturing, it doesn't have an ulterior motive – it isn't about pepping you up to the point of spun-out anxiety – but it has a worthy purpose: to be one of life's dependable chums. Coffee is percolated, tea is brewed – even by the appellation of its preparation, I know which is the drink that will make me feel better.

From tea that claims to support the breastfeeding process (Traditional Medicinals Mother's Milk and Weleda Nursing Tea) to the Chinese tradition of *yum cha* (tea served with dim sum), to the Indian ayurvedic practice of drinking herbal tea, the appeal of this humble beverage is universal and the permutations of the simple green leaf – once brewed – are vast. Whether it comes as the comforting milky masala chai sold by vendors on the streets of Varanasi in India, or the matcha sipped during an elegant Japanese Way of Tea ceremony (if you get the chance to attend one, it will, quite frankly, change your life), its global significance is undeniable, with cultures everywhere claiming the cosiness of tea and its properties as their own. There's green for cleansing, mint to aid digestion, camomile for de-stressing, and of course there are its thirst-quenching properties, mainly championed by my Bristolian nan Sylvia, who always proclaims to be parched when she comes in from shopping, at which point she reaches for not a glass of water, but the kettle.

Tea is home, tea is totally cosy and it belongs to us all.

How to make the perfect cup of tea

It's subjective, it's controversial and it will get you trolled on Twitter. Welcome to the world of asserting that you know how to make the perfect cup of tea. Choosing between leaf or bag is up to you – the rest should be as follows.

1. Step one begins with the water, and re-boiling is simply blasphe-tea. We've all done it and tolerated that metallic taste, but here's a life lesson you shouldn't ignore: when it comes to tea, shortcuts won't get you very far.

2. Now for the vessel. Those trendy lumberjack tin mugs are too hot to hold, plastic is just weird and,

while glass looks good, the hard, cool sides aren't cosy. Serving tea in a vintage porcelain cup might seem a little chintzy, but it's the proper thing to do.

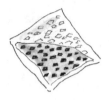

3. When it comes to the brew, two minutes is the optimum time for achieving a good, sturdy cup of black tea.

4. Add the milk, slowly stirring and daydreaming as you go, and then add sugar, unless you're sweet enough.

5. Biscuits are not optional.

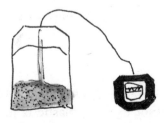

I love dressing for winter – I love how obvious it all is. There is no holiday wardrobe anxiety with winter clothes. Warm, layerable clothes know where they stand and what they require our bodies to do, and we just do what we are told. Our wardrobe's Ronseal, winter clothes don't require instructions, you pull them on with one objective: to stay warm, to be cosy. There are no bikini strings tickling your skin or flip-flops rubbing between your toes, no maxidress tummy bulges or jumpsuit wedgies. Winter clothes are practical, and quite right too. Instead of asking the mirror whether my bottom looks pert in this, it's, 'Will my extremities survive? Will I endure another winter commute? Will the soles of my shoes have my back as the frost descends on platform 6?'. It's also, 'Will I find a scarf long enough to do the triple neck wrap? Which winter coat will actually keep me warm and dry? And why do they never button all the way up?'.

The sheer weight of winter clothes makes us slow down. Come autumn, we are supposed to start disappearing under the duvet and getting a little bit fatter.

We shuffle to the shops in our winter wardrobes cloaked in eiderdowns; we tuck our pyjamas into our socks and pull our vests down to cover our kidneys and stave off the winter's inevitable, yet reassuringly bitter, chill. All this covering up isn't conducive to being sexy – if by sexy you mean less Scottish Highlands and more *Love Island*, but who cares?

Summer is marvellous. She's that stupidly gorgeous friend who floats around life's proverbial swimming pool atop an inflatable unicorn, all sun-kissed and brilliant, until you realise that, actually, she is a bit of a nightmare. Winter, you conclude, as the cloying heat of summer melts into autumn, is your warmest friend in the truest sense of the word. She isn't fleeting and temporary, she isn't only around for naïvely optimistic blue skies. Your good friend winter, wrapped up in cable-knit sweaters, hiking socks and corduroy, is here for the long haul, affectionately weathering the year's darkest days with you. She's newspapers and red wine, coal and cheese, she's long evenings and dark mornings. She's not a WhatsApp message, she's a phone call, and she looks bloody sexy in knitwear by candlelight.

The winter wardrobe, I like to think, pivots upon how slack we become with shaving our legs (and plucking our chins – I mean, what on earth are snoods for if not to hide hormonal facial hair?) as the first breaths of winter appear in October. I immediately retreat from any item of clothing that asks for effort and start to dress for myself. Most of what I wear as the mercury falls I put on out of laziness, as well as a desire to look as close to Cameron Diaz in *The Holiday* as humanly possible. But flannelette pyjamas are a thing, much to my immense pleasure, and so are sheepskin boots – in fact, all winter boots, which should be worn with chunky socks and long skirts, roll-neck sweaters and big knickers. These are clothes for the sleepy.

The irony is that the skimpiest of knickers are called 'intimates'. But there is nothing more intimate than being forced to hold someone close under the weight of a winter-tog duvet, basking in the oven of love that's keeping you warm because it feels like, without each other, your heart and soul might freeze.

Cosy toes

What is it about a pair of socks that gives them the divine status of 'most necessary piece of clothing in a wintry way'? Of course, winter coats and sweaters are up there on the cold-weather-staples list, but what are you without a pair of socks? Footloose and feckless, that's what. To wrap our feet in something tactile must send a positive message of comfort to the brain. To have one's feet exposed, the tender undersides of our soft trotters padding around on a cold floor during winter months, feels nothing but risky. Especially on the nail-strewn floorboards of a country cottage, or anywhere with children and Lego.

Once night falls, which is at about 4pm in the depths of winter, the first thing I and all my companions in cosy do is reach for a pair of evening socks. And these, as any cosyite will know, are different from your black multipack socks; they are usually a hiking sock or a slipper hybrid. In my mind, anyone who sleeps bare-foot in the winter is a psychopath. A reckless one. We step into our best shoes for a big night out, and I also put my best foot forward when I'm dressing to do nothing: with a good pair of socks on my feet, all is right with the world.

Whether yours are chunky ones from the high street, trendy ones from A Woven Plane, or made from Falke's finest cashmere, a thick pair of socks marks the end of the day; they're the full stop to your sofa flop. They are called cosy toes for a reason.

'I guess you could associate the desire for being swaddled in fabric with the growing fear for our safety or financial future. But like the hemline index that has always attributed long hemlines to an economic downturn, it's quite hard to verify with any degree of authority. From an anecdotal perspective, I would say yes. Plus last winter was fucking freezing.

I think everyone has a house trouser – probably tracksuit bottoms that should never see the light of day. A fat polo neck to hide in. A robe coat to tie up nice and tight. And slippers. Everyone needs slippers.'

**Jo Ellison, Fashion Editor
of the *Financial Times***

10 steps to cosy dressing

1. The sweater, or jumper, depending on how posh you are. Either way, it's a middle layer that goes the longest way.

2. Socks – as discussed, vital – and under no circumstances should you allow them to get wet.

3. Tights. Just don't (like my mum used to) wear knickers over the top to keep the crotch up. Just simply buy a pair that fit, the woollier the better.

4. A warm coat. This list follows no particular order, but a winter coat is a rite of passage into adulthood. When the days of you having to be rammed into a winter coat by your parents are replaced with you 'wanting' to put one on, you know that you are officially a grown-up.

5. Boots. Hobnail or wellie, lace-up or Chelsea – whatever your persuasion, a winter boot, hole free and of grippy sole, is necessary if you are to traverse the harsh British winter safely.

6. Hats are strange things, but nothing says 'I'm prepared' like a suitable headpiece. I go for a typical bobble or beanie, but I have been known to sport a leather Crocodile Dundee-style hat on autumn walks. Whatever your leaning, keep your noggin covered.

7. Gloves, or mittens (cute), are the best way to keep warm and to avoid frostbitten fingers. Plus, they provide a helpful nudge towards a digital detox, as scrolling through your smartphone's contents with a pair on becomes a challenge, to say the least.

8. Thermals – now you're talking. Big, old-people thermals say, 'I take the weather and my cosy game seriously'.

9. The knitted poncho. And out of left field here it comes, all hands free and warm torso – ideal for cosy camping.

10. Shawls. See almost every period drama, from *Braveheart* to *Little Women* (see page 143) shawls are there. It's not surprising – they're a clever layer, designed to close up any gaps and keep the warmth in and the cold out.

Winter and summer aren't just different seasons, they are different places to be: they require us to know ourselves in different ways. We shift our expectations to cater for one and then for the other, and although it happens every year, they always seem to arrive without enough notice. Achieving ultimate cosy is impossible unless there is the surprise of coldness in the morning. It certainly helps if cheeks are ruddy and glowing, if the wind is whipping, and crunching snow underfoot only adds to the situation. Of course, the primary ingredient – the only cosyfier that transcends both cold and warmth – is rain.

> *Here comes the rain again*
> *Falling on my head like a memory*

'Here Comes The Rain Again'
– Eurythmics

The more romcom the rain, the better the catalyst for cosy. I'm talking a downpour of the Andie MacDowell in *Four Weddings and a Funeral* proportions, only you

do notice it and it isn't soaking you through and drip-
ping off the end of your nose. You notice it because,
crucially, you are privileged enough to be inside. Under
cover, sheltered, lucky to be dry and warm and grateful
as the thunder crackles away above your tent, or the

raindrops tap on your tin roof (go with me), or hammer on your windowpane. Rainfall is a familiar and comforting sound for the 10 million of us who have listened to the most downloaded YouTube clip of 'rain sounds for sleeping', or for those who have tuned in to the tranquillising effects of rain when it is happening for real.

Sometimes the rain hits the earth in big drops – juicy, wet punches that cling to our skin – and other days it sprays down like a burst bag of rice. And then there are the sheets of relentless, life-affirming rain (my favourite kind) that render you defenceless and force you to take cover. As a country we are divided about so many things, but the one thing that unites us is having an opinion about the weather.

There are some of you who worship the sun – cold bemoaners, who pejoratively tut, 'Oh, it's raining again,' as you pull up your hoods and look to the sky, blaming its wonder for your ills. And while it's unlikely you are reading this book (I can't imagine that seeking the condolence of cosy is up your street if you don't like it being nippy), I do understand. You enjoy the kick up the bum that comes from the sun. The jolt of vitamin D, the lollies and sticky chins, the wasps and bees, your toes dipping in things like sand and the sea, the tanned décolletés and beer-belly midriffs out for everyone to see. The streaks of fake tan and the burnt tops of heads, the sunhats, factor 50 and faces that are lobster red. The barbecues and picnics (though those can be cosy, too) and the being outside for as long as you want to be. Headline-worthy heatwaves, the sweat, the odour and the melting, too, the eggs frying on tarmac and arthritic joints easing in the sun.

But once the sun has taken off his hat and vanished and we are left with the regularity of the rain, it's far better to light a fire and warm up that way, wouldn't you say? I think we should be appreciative of the extremities of our little island's condition and the cosiness and part-time hibernation it affords us. I like my weather with edge and variety. Who wants thick, monosyllabic sunshine beating down upon us all the time? This is the northern hemisphere, we aren't equipped.

When summer ends, I start again. I've typically spent the first six months of the year on Instagram wishing I was on holiday, and then wishing I hadn't spent so much time on Instagram while I was on holiday, because summer is over now and it's never coming back. So when autumn arrives I vow never to make the same mistake, not until next summer at least. As I stand at the foot of a new season and start to feel the breeze on my skin, the chill in my bones, it feels like I'm alive for the first time in the year. Sunlight soothes, but brisk air and crisp skies bring a jolt of energising chill to life.

The feeling that cosy is truly setting in and bedding down in its proverbial sleeping bag, lands quietly like gentle snowfall as the clocks go back an hour in

October and the daylight suddenly disappears. The leaves have changed colour, from green to golden brown and russet and red, and because England is old, and/or the streets are brilliantly knackered, the fallen leaves carpet the ground before creating a brown autumnal sludge which cakes the remnants of British cobbled streets from London and Bath to the Isle of Bute and beyond. A different light arrives, a bit more golden in the cool sunlight, a bit sharper after the rain, and my sense of being reborn for winter usually starts a week ahead of the 5th of November. That is when I begin the process of drawing inwards, stop dwelling on the past of long summer days and face up to it: winter is here.

My Bonfire Night preparations begin with the plotting of where to stare into the flames and watch the action; sometimes that's making the journey to Lewes in Sussex to see an effigy of whichever politician has rubbed the zeitgeist up the wrong way getting burnt on a stake; and sometimes it's staying at home with the TV tuned to 'flames'. But usually I opt to visit friends in the countryside who have a garden-type field and tons of children. They light a huge bonfire, and even if it's 15°C, we all insist on wearing our hats, scarves and gloves for the first time that season, and I spend most of the evening worrying about the hedgehogs in the wood pile, who most certainly live there, or did, anyway.

Bringing out the winter accessories signals that you have surrendered to being reliant on something or someone to protect you. It's not like summer, when a pair of pants and a bottle of SPF will suffice. Winter calls for all hands on deck, layers, barriers, survival. And whether your Bonfire Night festivities include being in a muddy field, in a city park, or on an apartment rooftop, from the 5th of November (if not before) a winter coat (see page 18) is entirely necessary, too.

Food at this time of year starts with jacket potatoes and ends in baked beans, and we live this way, on a strict, unvaried diet of stodge and cosy, until we open the virgin window of our supermarket advent calendars on the 1st of December.

COSY CRAFTING

COSY CRAFTING

'The hand is the window on to the mind'
Immanuel Kant, philosopher

While trundling along a towpath in Hackney, East London, recently – the capital's hip heartland, I saw an advert for a 'flat-pack man', a bloke you can pay to assemble your flat-pack furniture for you. It's an ironic development, given that the romanticising of hand made craftsmanship by the under forties is on the rise. Whether it's whittling spoons while dressed in leather aprons, brewing your own craft ale, or smoking a fillet of trout on a bed of Welsh wood and then throwing the pottery plate that you'll eat it off, the primitive idea of making things with our hands has become completely contemporary as we retrench and realise we must be able to rely on ourselves. It might sound niche and small scale, but at the last count, the UK has managed to build this into a £3.4 billion sector[1].

In fact, in the British Isles we are blessed with a legacy of incredibly cosy crafts. It is written into our DNA that, as the winter's frost and cold clusters of icicles curtain our windows, we get the knitting needles out, start the pottery wheel spinning, set the loom going and get knitting and weaving and creating.

Welsh weaving is one such trend, its product a timeless textile that has recently made a comeback, thanks to its signature geometric patterns in bright, unconventional colour combinations. Using looms to achieve the double weave that makes the blankets durable and extra-cosy, Welsh weavers have long been aware of the well-being benefits of their profession: studies show knitting and weaving can reduce blood pressure, reduce depression[2] and improve brain power. Although we no longer 'need' to make these things, we would do well to remember that manmade is not the same as handmade. These crafts feed our soul. They keep us human and keep us useful. Is doing the crossword a craft? It should be.

Fair Isle
Picture a patterned knitted sweater, the posh kind, often to be found moth-eaten in rural charity shops or slung over shoulders on London's Sloane Street. The intricate motifs of Fair Isle sweaters – usually some kind of diamond paired with a zigzag – made popular

by King Edward VIII and iconic by Sarah Lund in cult Nordic noir film *The Killing*, tell tales of nature, religion and human emotion. From rams' heads to leaves, anchors' horns and hearts, the tiny community of Fair Isle, in remote Scotland, continues to knit using symbols, with waiting lists for a true Fair Isle jumper, complete with the signature colours and patterns, more than three years long.

Aran Islands

Traditionally made with untreated and washed sheep's wool to preserve the lanolin and thus make it water-proof, the Aran knit is the daddy of jumpers. Whether found on Cornish fishermen or the catwalks of Paris, its cosy charm is as unsurpassed as its stylish appeal. Usually made in off-white or cream, this provides any cosy-jumper collection with a dreamy neutral staple.

Channel Islands

Legend has it that Mary, Queen of Scots wore a pair of knitted Guernsey stockings for her execution. Hardy, seafaring sorts, Channel Island fishermen know their knitwear, and the traditional characteristics of a Guernsey jumper include slits at the side to allow for greater movement.

Q&A with Jade Harwood, co-founder and creative director of knitting brand, Wool and the Gang

Wool and the Gang is the DIY fashion brand that started a knitting revolution with its kits and worldwide community of crafters, simultaneously transforming the image of cosy living in the process.

Why Knitting?

I was a really nerdy child and was into knitting from the age of seven. My nan taught me how to knit on those tiny metal needles that took a lifetime to make anything. I went to Central Saint Martins where I specialised in textiles, and met my buddy Aurelie Popper, who is one of the co-founders of Wool and the Gang. Aurelie introduced me to the fabulous ex-model, Lisa Sabrier who had the original idea to make knitting cool, fun, sexy and fast, and break the image that knitting had. That's where the madness started.

What's the concept behind Wool and the Gang?

It's a DIY fashion brand. We've always been passionate about sustainability and for us, being part of the DIY-making experience has so many positive effects:

it helps you relax and it lowers stress levels. Our customers can cherish the product they've made; whether they gift it to someone or keep it for themselves it creates a rush of happiness.

Why do you think there's been a renaissance in knitting?

I think it's definitely a reaction to the digital world. After the Industrial Revolution, the Arts and Crafts Movement came as a reaction to it and this is similar. People want to go back to basics, connect to the real world and to get off their phones – basically to have a digital detox and to do something creative with their time, other than binge-watch Netflix. Knitting has a meditative pull – I need to knit in order to unwind after a crazy day.

What are the brand's key cosy pieces?

I feel like a blanket is the ultimate cosy thing to knit, especially using our Crazy Sexy wool, which is soft, chunky and easy to knit with.

What tips would you give someone who has never knitted before?

Go for chunky wool and chunky needles – the size and scale of the knit give instant gratification and encouragement. Chunky wool is also more forgiving of mistakes. The perfect first project is definitely a scarf.

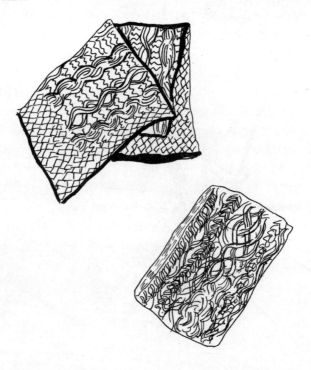

COSY FEASTS

Is there anything less cosy than a salad? And, equally, anything more satisfying than hot, buttered, freshly sliced white toast dipped in stew? Or anything drowning in gravy, for that matter? How about your nan's cottage pie, your girlfriend's reassuringly stodgy spag bol, or your beloved biscuit of choice dunked in a cup of tea?

A married couple I know have a signature dish; it's called reassuring ratatouille. It's the meal they have cooked for one another when they have been unceremoniously sacked from their jobs, and which they now wheel out in any emotional emergency. Food is intrinsically attached to our memories, so it stands to reason that cosy food warms us inside. There's mashed potato (nothing cosier), goat curry with rice and peas on a wet London day, apple crumble and custard (lumpy or not), cake and a cuppa, tomato soup and buttered brown bread, a can of beans and sausages warmed over a Calor-gas camping stove. There's hot steaming porridge, a bowl of creamy dhal and rice, Irish stew, and chicken pie (with gravy) and, of course, a Sunday roast. There's cosiness in routine and pattern, and a Sunday roast is something upon which we can all rely.

But what is it that makes some items of food – some dishes and culinary constructions – innately cosy and comforting, and other foods, well, just not so much? A cool sushi roll or a deeply uncomforting slice of melon guides us to the answer. The key contributor to comfort-food credentials is, I think, temperature. Cold food cannot be cosy, and other key ingredients for staving off the sterile and ushering in the warmth include a healthy appetite, not being on any kind of diet and talking as you eat. There is also a ritualistic pleasure to the cooking of hot food. Being forced to wait patiently for your feast to be ready is a chance to steal a moment, tune into your belly rumble and focus on the slow rhythm of chopping or stirring as your mouth begins to ache and salivate at the thought of what's about to arrive. 'If anyone does not have three minutes in his life to make an omelette, then life is not worth living,' says the chef Raymond Blanc, and he's right.

Recipes for a cosy dinner

My nan's cottage pie

There's no garlic, no tomato purée or any fancy stuff in this, it's nan cooking: simple, delicious and cosy.

Serves 1, 2 or 4 depending on how greedy you are

1 large onion
3 tbsp butter and a dash of oil
1kg minced beef (beef for cottage; lamb for shepherd's)
1 OXO cube
sprinkling of gravy granules
4 large potatoes
a dash of full fat milk
a pinch or two of salt
a sprinkle of pepper

Peel and chop the onion – a teaspoon in the mouth doesn't work; just do it quickly.

Put 2 tablespoons of the butter and a dash of oil (Nan uses sunflower, or olive oil is an option) in a pan and heat on the stove until melted but not smoking. Add the onion and cook until glassy.

Add the mince and cook until brown, but not quite all the way through, then add the OXO cube, a couple of tablespoons of water, a sprinkling of gravy granules and bring to a simmer, then take off the heat.

Meanwhile, heat your oven to 160°C (Gas Mark 3). Peel and chop your potatoes and boil until mashable. Mash them, adding the final tablespoon of butter and a dash of full fat milk, then season with salt and pepper.

Pop the meat in a shallow baking dish and cover with the mash, then fork the top with wiggly lines for effect. Bake for 25 minutes, until the top is crispy. Serve with a smile.

Apple crumble

A classic, a crumble feels cosier than a pie. Best served with custard, of course (I buy mine in a shop).

Serves 4 gannets or 6 people of average appetite

4 large cooking apples
120g sugar (I like brown but caster is an option)
150g flour (plain is best)
80g butter

Peel, core and chop the apples into chunks – they shouldn't be too big so that they can sweat.

Put them into a pan with a couple of spoonfuls of water and half of the sugar and stew them until they are a sweet, mushy consistency. Heat your oven to 170°C (Gas Mark 3).

Take the flour, butter and remaining sugar and mix them with your fingertips until the mixture becomes cleggy and crumbly. Put the stewed apple into a shallow dish and scatter the crumble mix on top. Add a little sprinkle of extra sugar and bake for about 40 minutes.

An ode to comfort food by Jeremy Lee, chef proprietor of Quo Vadis, London

'In the kitchen a great pan of lentil soup simmers, a ham hock gently softening in among much potato and carrot and lentils to make a soup that has nourished body and soul against the wild, deep chill of the northern lands since as far back as I can remember. A loaf, warmed in the oven to ensure a fine crust, served up with good butter is all that is required to create the feeling of warmth and irresistible cosiness that I learnt at my mother's knee. Her much-loved face would peek around the door and enquire, with a familiar grin, if her brood, "were a'cosy".

The food that has folk rushing to the table in the days when the nights draw in early is comforting and nourishing, soothing and warming. Great pans of broth or soup fit this bill beautifully. The other great contender is a pie: pieces of meats of one kind or a goodly mix such as differing birds or game and beef. A beautiful braise, a fine pastry crust, be it flaky or suet, and of course, a great bowl of piping-hot mashed potatoes is a feast that's hard to beat.

A friend has a mother who used to make a steamed suet pudding stuffed full of leeks that kicked in a craving with alarming zeal.

Cosy foods may well be defined by recipes handed down through generations, recipes that are fondly remembered from eating with grandparents or old friends who cooked plain and simple, unfussy foods made from good produce that had flavours most memorable. These memories – I am blessed with many – were sparked when crossing the threshold into a home whose air was rich with the scents and smells of good home cooking. Pity the tub of Ben & Jerry's against a homemade apple pie and fresh egg custard.

Comfort and cosy is rarely to be found sealed in plastic in a box, these being foods that fuel out of necessity and lack of time. Cosy and comfort is made with time stolen in the kitchen; the phone switched off, the laptop gathering dust, television in the bin and only the thought of a gathering of chums, perhaps, who may also just want a bowl of soup.

And soup they shall have.'

Cosy tipples

There's nothing like warming the cockles with a giant glass of something hot. Here are my recommendations:

1. Slightly warm red wine is the best on a winter's eve. Open a bottle and sit it by the fire (or balance it on the radiator) for added comfort and drinkability.

2. Mulled anything – cider, wine . . . I'd mull my own arm if I could. The blend of herbs and heat is ideal.

3. Whiskey or whisky, preferably taken as a hot toddy, is as grounding as it is potent.

4. Hot Ribena. 'Hot Beena, Mummy. Hot Beena.' That was me, aged three, having been weaned off milk and thirsty for the most comforting drink known to man – hot Ribena. It was the Eighties, and sugar wasn't poisonous yet. Later in life – 20 years later in fact – me and my flatmate, the now famous Mancunian model and actress Agyness Deyn, used to cosy up in our flat in West Hampstead and drink what she called 'hot cordial' in a Northern twang. The cosy properties of a sweet sugar syrup warmed with boiling water and drunk while huddled around a radiator are undeniable.

5. Hot chocolate (also, a cup of cocoa, a mug of Horlicks at a push). The chocolate releases endorphins into the brain and happy hormones too. Then comes the comforting sweetness and the indulgent texture. Liquid love.

6. Milk. Often demonised but I have a lot of love for this egalitarian, reassuring liquor. A mug of warm milk soothes many a cosy soul; it can settle an anxious stomach, builds bones and takes us straight back to childhood, picking up where the bosom or bottle left off.

My cosiest foodie feelings, by Melissa Hemsley, food writer and author

'You say cosy, I say comfort foods. Foods you can eat with a bowl and spoon and the type of comforting that is deliciously nurturing, restorative and just full enough but not stuffed, sluggish and drained! The great thing about cosy comfort foods is that they taste best in big portions, with little fuss and made ahead.

If I'm struggling or feeling out of sorts, my number one thing to do to feel a bit better is to make a giant pot of something. The easiest is a soup, blend it if you can be bothered, but sometimes extra washing up ain't worth it. The other thing I do is make a Bolognese, everything simmers for at least 4 hours, I grate as much veg in as I can, and I know I'm guaranteed a great stretch of reading time in the bath before dinner whilst it's bubbling away. I'm talking big batches of creamy fish pie topped with sweet potato mash or storecupboard staple veggie lentil pies with a quick cheesy cauliflower mash. Double up and make double portions (sticking one in the freezer for a rainy day) or if you're feeling extra angelic, make a triple portion and give one to your neighbour - it's food karma! Next time they make some cookies or banana bread, they'll probably make extra for you.

When the weather isn't friendly, you'll be happy your freezer is full and your cupboards are stocked up – an investment to your busy future self. Like a Spring Clean, give your kitchen an Autumn revamp and have a big shop of bulk goods. You'll save time, money and even better, bulk ordering means less plastic and packaging all round.

I love the Autumn as it encourages what I call 'granny dinners' (early evening suppers) which for me means an earlier bedtime (plus better digestion). It gives you the chance to have more time on the sofa with a sleepy brew – maybe a super relaxing almond milk warmed up with lavender and chamomile or a creamy mug of hot chocolate with full fat milk. The best.'

Whether your home is humble or hefty, shabby chic, or flashy, or bleak: your home is your castle, your domain, your space. As the world outside our window becomes more unpredictable, the notion of hunkering down in a sanctuary that we can control amidst the chaos has a covetous appeal. According to design expert Dr Vanessa Brady, founder of the Society of British and International Design, interior design contributes £11.6 billion a year to the UK economy, as we all buy into the idea that our homes are an extension of who we are and how we want to be perceived. Whether you're a minimalist or a maximalist the idea of bringing cosiness into our homes appeals to most people I know – a home without a feeling of cosy is just a museum. Creating a cosy space that feels like your haven on earth isn't going to solve the world's problems, but it's a good place to start.

'A cosy home to me is one that is layered and rich with textures and styles. A home should be inviting – it's far more welcoming squishing yourself into an already dented sofa than having to place your bum delicately on the edge so not to intrude on some immaculately puffed cushions. It should be personal – it's all in the details – the items picked up on a memorable holiday, trinkets given by friends – these memories lined up along your mantelpiece or squeezed into the edge of a mirror are priceless and something that are acclimated over time. Get rid of those overhead spotlights and opt for lots of varying styles of lighting; think about placing lamps in unconventional places such as the counter worktop of a kitchen or low hanging pendant lights draped into a corner to read. Think about adding art and even adding a small armchair or table into your bathroom. A wallpapered bathroom is heaven and often a less daunting room to use a print.'

Matilda Goad, interior designer

Cosy lighting

Ah, the joy of the dimly lit room! If I had my way, my entire world would be eternally – and subtly – shone upon by warm, flickering candlelight. My busy dinner table would be illuminated by twinkling lights, and my bath would be lit by no more than a lantern. There are people who seek out bright light – think about the high-octane celebrity who revels in the flashbulbs; they're not called stars just because they shine brighter than the rest of us – they love to bathe in the limelight. And then cast your mind towards the recluse. I am truly at my happiest when buried in a slanket on the sofa much more so than at a premiere or party.

A log fire, a large glass of red wine and a pair of slipper socks don't have the same comforting qualities when rendered luminous under harsh strip lighting. The essence of being cosy is about making our surroundings as soothing as possible. My well-being definitely increases as the wattage of the room gets turned down.

My favourite kind of kitchens are those that bustle with low level lighting, the best dining tables are wooden and dotted with melted wax, and nothing says 'Haven't they done well?' like twizzling your friends' dimmer switches when you walk into their new home. Choosing one's ambient lighting is the ultimate luxury – just ask Sir Paul McCartney, who reportedly insists that all lamps backstage are halogen floor lamps with dimmer switches. And then there's Rihanna, who apparently requires 'adequate lighting for a relaxed atmosphere' – she's a woman after my own heart[3].

The best way to ruin a home is with bad lighting, as is the best way to kill a mood or shatter an illusion. We are hard-wired to respond to bright lights with an energised response. A candle, on the other hand, casts a subtle light: as the flame flutters, it creates a gentle atmosphere of low productivity. When one is lit, it warms the heart and signals that the time has come to rest easy.

If the flattering glow of candlelight isn't enough to switch you on to low lighting or, you're simply adverse to the obvious fire risks; there are also health benefits to turning the big light off. Bright light, particularly the blue light that gadgets and some energy-efficient light bulbs throw out, has a dark side. According to Harvard Medical School, being in bright light at night throws the human circadian rhythm out of whack and can disrupt the production of melatonin (the good-sleep hormone), so a late-night social-media scroll wires up the brain to inter-act rather than settle down. It may not feel like you're living at the bleeding edge of cool, but a grip-ping bedtime book accompanied by a 40-watt bulb in a lamp is where it's at[4].

'For me, without question, the most important thing in a home is cosiness. It's about books and lights, cushions, pale pinks and leopard print, pictures and mementos, and all the rest; evidence of you and what you love and who you all are that live there.'

Bay Garnett, fashion stylist

Setting the scene

In the world of interior design, layering light is the only way to create atmosphere in a room. Think about how, for centuries, Christian churches have combined different lighting designs to achieve maximum celestial rousing. From the sunlight that streams through high stained-glass windows, to the candles at eye height, wall lamps that shine down on the congregation, and the central (usually enormous) chandelier that projects the grandeur of Him upstairs. Mosques are built around a skylit atrium to allow the light of Allah to flood into the building, with floor-level lighting, lamps and lanterns adding to the atmosphere. Hindu temples embrace the art of candlelight and the festival of Diwali is devoted to the power of light. In our homes, the kind of lighting we choose reflects back at us the atmosphere we want to live in. Here are my top three:

1. Candles
The light of a candle is, quite literally, divine. The flame represents the source of our creation and staring into it for a minute or two is just as relaxing as unhooking my bra after an 18-hour day. I have an

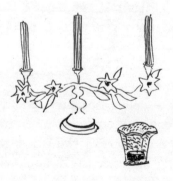

unhealthy addiction to scented candles: Maria Santa Novella's Rosa is the stuff of dreams, while the decorative pots of Fornasetti candles and the modern quirk of Matilda Goad's Crayola-coloured beeswax ribbed candles are all pretty lit (ahem). There is something noble and pure about a tea light, or a stocky church candle. In fact, there are times when burning beeswax without a scent is a good idea: it encourages us to appreciate the light, rather than alerting our senses to the smell, which can be a distraction.

2. Bedside lamps

There's something so BHC (British Home Counties) about the bedside lamp duo. There they are, the pair of them, standing – nay, peering – all sexless and reliable, matching each other from their own side of the bed, waiting while the human settles down with her good book to come into their own. The brands Pooky and Fermoie create my favourite lamps, serving up decorative lampshades and arty bases that combine countryside sensibilities with a stylish twist.

3. The hearth

If you're lucky enough to have an open fire you know the drill. First comes the sheer triumph of lighting it from just a handful of rolled-up pages of *Grazia* magazine and a slightly damp box of matches. Up next is your signature Bear Grylls blow – it's an 'I'm an expert', gentle, long-winded puff that keeps the embers glowing until the kindling bites and flares. Then it's time for the loading of the logs – not so many that they suffocate the flames, but just enough to keep them chasing the oxygen, a couple of lumps of coal for posterity, and then aahhhhhhh. Feet up, box turned on, glass of wine poured and . . . relax . . . wait . . . I'm boiling, can you open the window?

'By an Autumn Fire'
by Lucy Maud Montgomery

Now at our casement the wind is shrilling,
Poignant and keen
And all the great boughs of the pines between
It is harping a lone and hungering strain
To the eldritch weeping of the rain;
And then to the wild, wet valley flying
It is seeking, sighing,

Something lost in the summer olden.
When night was silver and day was golden;
But out on the shore the waves are moaning
With ancient and never fulfilled desire,
And the spirits of all the empty spaces,
Of all the dark and haunted places,
With the rain and the wind on their death-white faces,
Come to the lure of our leaping fire.

But we bar them out with this rose-red splendour
From our blithe domain,
And drown the whimper of wind and rain
With undaunted laughter, echoing long,
Cheery old tale and gay old song;
Ours is the joyance of ripe fruition,
Attained ambition.
Ours is the treasure of tested loving,
Friendship that needs no further proving;

No more of springtime hopes, sweet and uncertain,
Here we have largesse of summer in fee
Pile high the logs till the flame be leaping,
At bay the chill of the autumn keeping,
While pilgrim-wise, we may go a-reaping
In the fairest meadow of memory!

Crackling wood fires are the cosiest of cosy, and as the great debate of whether wood burners in the home are resident evil, and the love affair with the fireplace seems to be cooling for some, I strike my matches resolutely on. For early humans, the hypnotic fireside, or fire's edge, provided warmth, warded off predators, illuminated dark places and facilitated cooking, and it continues to do so. In my front room, I protect myself against the proverbial predators (that bus driver who splashed me with a puddle, or the colleague who ruined my day) and illuminate the darker side of my mood with a fire. I don't use it for cooking, but it does extend the day as it would have done for earlier civilisations, especially in the darker winter months.

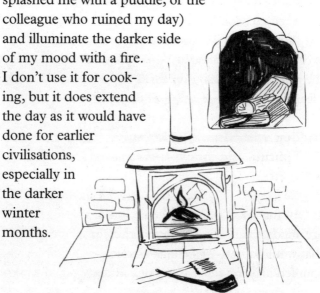

Yes, fires can be inefficient and polluting, and among the environmentally responsible, wood burning is earning the same stigma as single-use plastic or smoking – according to health professionals, wood smoke contains some of the same particulars as cigarettes – but to me, being a fire-naysayer is like saying you can't enjoy the countryside for fear of getting mown down by a tractor: it's eco-overkill. I'd rather lower my carbon emissions by turning the heating off and occasionally lighting my fire, safe in the knowledge that I don't own a car and I recycle fastidiously. Core values of the pursuit of cosy are not to take yourself too seriously and to do everything in moderation. Somehow, lighting a fire – the most natural thing on earth – has become a guilty pleasure. But it's a pleasure all the same.

Ridden with flaming-hot guilt? Try these tips for lighting and enjoying fire super-responsibly and getting eco-cosy:

1. Opt for wood pellets – they're harder to source but are made from sawdust and other timber materials that would otherwise be lingering in landfill; or locally sourced logs, rather than treated and imported wood.

2. Get your fireplace checked for cracks or damage that could add to the pollutants escaping.

3. Make sure your firewood is dry as wet logs create more smoke. Slam two logs together: if they are dry they will sound like a bat hitting a cricket ball, rather than a thud.

'I love cashmere so much I wear it in summer! I would go as far as saying that it epitomises cosiness. My favourite and most loved Christopher Kane cashmere scarf travels everywhere with me, it was made by Johnstons in Scotland. I have no idea what their secret is but I think it's the best in the world – it is beyond soft and cuddly. There is nothing like being at home on a cold day with the fire on, cashmere-ed up to my eyeballs watching TV on the couch with my boyf and Bruce, my dog. BLISS!'

Fashion designer Christopher Kane

Blankets

I can chart and track my short life through my blanket collection. For my 18th birthday, when friends who were massively cooler than me were getting new cars, I asked my parents for a hand-spun blanket (it was as itchy as hell) in multicoloured patchwork from a farm shop we ended up in while on a camping trip. Years later whilst pregnant I craved a cosy blanket that I could permanently retreat under, and bought an enormous throw that I wrapped around myself. I wore it throughout my wintry maternity leave and when I brought my daughter home from hospital it became a tent for two. Then, last autumn, I discovered Begg & Co, and in doing so, arrived at my blanket nirvana by way of the most exquisite lambswool cashmere throw that exists on planet earth, woven in the company's mill in Scotland.

I love my patchwork blanket like nothing else I have ever owned. I have cried under it, loved under it, snuggled under it and slept under it. I've wrapped my daughter in it and taken my cat to the vet in it. My emotions are woven into it, and it's never been washed, so it does actually smell of life. Storing it became a project of its own: a blanket box-meets-picnic basket is where it has ended up. Despite the twee connotations, it really is the best home for it, and having all of my blankets at my fingertips is the ultimate in cosy convenience.

'I believe the super-fast pace of modern society requires an antidote, and more than ever it requires a slower aspect to create a balance. Home becomes a sanctuary. Simple pleasures like blankets become luxurious.'

**Lorraine Acornley, Creative Director
of blanket brand Begg & Co**

Central heating

There's a house at the bottom of Primrose Hill in North London, a large period townhouse, the type into whose bedroom Peter Pan might fly, and in its big bay window at the front, there was, for many years, a dapple-grey rocking horse. At Christmas time I used to walk past it and romanticise about living in a house like that with a family of my own one day. They don't have to turn the big light off and scrimp on heating bills, I thought.

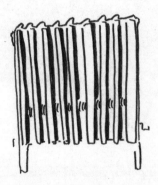

It's in December, as the winter chill begins to set into our bones, that we start to think about the prospect of never being able to warm up. You see, fancy meals and fast cars are fleetingly brilliant, but a toasty house and a pouffe to rest one's weary legs on for eternity? Now you're cooking with gas. It's probably why, at Christmas time, our minds and thoughts turn to those who are less fortunate than ourselves, those who might be cold, lonely, hungry or without those things that make modern life bearable.

COSY AND KIND

Somewhere in the folds of being cosy is the idea that we are incredibly lucky to be so. As I was writing this book, I realised that although in its purest state a sense of cosy is simple to achieve, in its essence it is about a state of the human condition, caveman stuff really, a way of living which eschews greed and materialism for good homely things. But there are elements, like a roof over your head, a blanket, a pair of lovely socks, which turbocharge the concept, and to have those is to be fortunate. It's not elitist for us to celebrate cosy culture, in the same way that Italians champion their *bella figura* lifestyle. Cosy is a way of life. Yet for some living cosily, and living comfortably, could come a little easier. The segue between being cosy and kind is the idea of warmth. Whether it's the kind of storybook type of love that radiates from a giving heart, actual 'I can now feel my fingers and toes' toastiness, having a full and settled stomach or being around loving company, being cosy feels like a human right. So if we are celebrating the privilege of being cosy, and the blessings it brings us, we should try to help others feel that too.

Be cosy and kind, you know you want to:

1. Donate a coat. Whether you hand one out yourself, hand one in to a charity shop or leave one in a dry place where you know someone cold is likely to seek shelter, to give a coat to someone who needs it is noble and kind.

2. Become the stealth de-icer: rise early and chuck down de-icing solution on the drives and steps of your elderly neighbours' homes. They don't need to know, but you will.

3. Take a neighbour, young or old, some soup. Couch the gesture by pretending that you made far too much and they would be doing you a huge favour by taking some from you.

4. Knit and knit and knit some more, if you know how to do it. Do it for a good cause – that good cause could be a homeless person's frozen fingers.

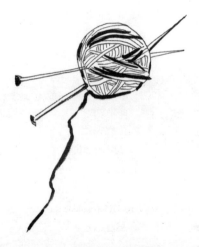

And if you want to do a little bit more, there are a few brilliant charities with cosiness at the heart of all they do . . .

Knit for Peace

Knit for Peace brings together women from traditionally hostile communities to knit clothes for children
and orphans. After the charity began, volunteers
from the UK started to ask if they could also make
donations. They now have over 22,000 volunteers.

The Bristol Soup Run Trust

Bristol has a huge homeless population with 1 in 170
people being classed as homeless. Every night this
charity makes sure
that as many as
20 different
groups
deliver
hot food/
supplies/infor-
mation (such as where
to go for shelter etc.)
to the homeless in
Bristol.

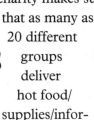

The Great Get Together

The Great Get Together was inspired by the late politician Jo Cox. The charity believes there is a groundswell of people who reject divisive politics and simply want to bring communities together and celebrate all that unites us. They suggest holding tea mornings or baking for your neighbours to bring the community together and raise funds.

Project Linus

Dedicated area co-ordinators organise sewing and fundraising events across the UK, as well as liaising with and distributing quilts and blankets to local hospitals, children's hospices, women's refuges, foster carers, bereavement services and many other places where support is given to children 'in need of a hug'.

Loving Hands

The ethos behind Loving Hands is to bring together like-minded crafters to knit, crochet and sew for charities and groups from all over the world. Through careful vetting Loving Hands makes sure that every charity, group or individual they recommend is taking the items directly to the areas of most need and hand delivering them to the people in crisis or animals in need.

Macmillan: The World's Biggest Coffee Morning

The World's Biggest Coffee Morning is Macmillan's biggest fundraising event for people facing cancer. The charity asks people all over the UK to host their own coffee mornings and donations on the day are made to Macmillan. In 2017 alone they raised over £27 million.

The Big Knit

As many as 200,000 older people say they haven't spoken to friends or family for over a month. The hats on Innocent smoothies raise money for activities at local Age UK centres where older people can get together for things like lunches and dance classes. The Big Knit started back in 2003 with Innocent asking some people – both young and old – to knit little woolly hats. They put those hats on their smoothies, and for each one sold made a donation of 25p to Age UK. The idea snowballed and so far around 6 million hats have been knitted, raising over £2 million for Age UK.

The Royal Navy & Royal Marines Children's Fund

The only charity dedicated to supporting children whose parents work for the naval services, it looks for knitters to volunteer their time and spare wool to create small dolls.

Francis House

Francis House Children's Hospice offers the families of very sick children a respite from their role as carers and gives the children a loving home from home. Each year handmade toys are made to help raise funds.

COSY SELF-CARE

The stresses of everyday life have become the background narrative to our daily output. Even the most pleasurable moments – like sharing a Sunday lunch with friends – have become plagued by our phone battery dying, making sure we catch that delayed train home, or knowing that the working week is looming. With anxiety levels at an all-time high, bringing some cosy into our self-care routines is key to making sure that we're not shortchanging ourselves by forgetting to find moments of cosy calm in the simplest of daily doings.

Growing up I longed for a shower – what I thought of as a fantastically fangled, standalone residential waterfall was a thing of dreams for me. I was raised on baths and bathing, and to this day there is a broken shower in my family home and so my mum sinks into the tub every evening.

It's not the most economical way of washing, but having a bath is about so much more than being clean, it's about relaxing and winding down. It's where I think, it's where my sister Jess watches her tablet and catches up on box sets (we aren't all in there together I might add) and I'm not sure there's anything better than eating a bowl of pasta in the bath. Not to mention the sedative effects of bathing. If I am struggling with sleep, a hot bath followed by a magnesium vitamin tablet and I'm away. I have climbed into a bath at 7pm and got out at 10pm. I scroll through my Instagram and read books – is there anything more civilised? And then there's the ritual. Lie for a bit, dunk my head for a bit and stay submerged listening to the sound of the bath.

Part meditation and part listening exercise, sound baths are the latest well-being craze: healing musical performances played with metal bowls and chanting; but really we've all been sound bathing since we were kids, holding our breath and seeing how long we could stay under water – muffling out the noise of the world outside.

The key to the optimum bath, according to experts, is getting the temperature right: 40°C is regarded to be the perfect temperature. Anything higher can cause you to overheat, triggers your fight or flight response and makes you want to jump out. And that warm water needs to be more than just a tub of liquid: make it work hard, use aromatherapy oils, and bubble bath to amplify your soak. There's the traditional bright green pine scented Wiberg's bubble bath, found in aristo homes across the country, there's designer bath oils like those from Aromatherapy Associates there's Radox for an eighties moment or there's bubble bath – I love Neal's Yard.

Studies show that some essential oils can enhance our state of well-being. Try petitgrain and grapefruit for a bracing soak, a concoction that lends itself to a bath designed more to clean than to calm. Mega stressed? Try lavender and eucalyptus, or bergamot. And if you're feeling a tad emotional and vulnerable this is where the cosy properties of camomile and jasmine come in. Ease your tired body with salts – I buy cheap and cheerful magnesium salts from the local chemist.

'For me taking a bath is about so much more than being clean,' says beauty expert, Rose Beer. 'Since starting my working life a daily wallow in water has become an essential ritual that signifies the end of the working day – a literal divider between my public and my private life and a process that undoubtedly bene-fits both my physical and mental well-being. It's a way of thinking universally acknowledged elsewhere in the world. In Japan, for example, bathing is an integral and widely celebrated part of daily life.'

Once suitably bathed, don't neglect a stolen moment at the sink. Is it only me who finds the routine act of brush-ing my teeth at the sink immensely comforting and cosy on a cold winter's evening? Much like other parts of our lives that have become increasingly automated and mechanised, the simple task of washing our faces has been eclipsed by the disposable ease of face wipes and cleaners. I am making a case for a return to washing my face over the sink. Old school, yes, am I making too much of it? Probably, but if it means me taking another few moments for myself at the end of the day I'm into it. I find washing my face almost cathartic, transportative even. The motion of splashing my face with water over and over again is meditative, and washing my face with a smooth liquid face wash is so satisfying.

Elsewhere on the list of tedious tasks that we can trans-form into cosy musings is applying our war paint. According to a recent survey 67 per cent of women travelling to work in cities apply their make-up on their commute, so many in fact that cosmetics companies are creating portable on-the-go solutions: fingertip eyeliner, for example, to cater for those looking to build shortcuts into their daily routine. I am advocating taking the time to be a bit more mindful about our make-up. Sales of colouring books that calm the minds of stressed-out adults have been on the rise, so why not de-stress and cosy up by colouring in your face? Get out of the bath, wrap up in a dressing gown, sit in front of the radiator and start your masterpiece.

Cosy crystals

Hijacked by hipsters and poached by influencers, the way in which we perceive the power of crystals is polarised. They have either been written off as hippy dippy constructs or they are being embraced with an open heart by a new generation of healer-seekers. So how do crystals relate to being cosy? The means of being cosy is conducive to being in a comfortable state of well-being, and there are certain crystals that are said to promote these settled, more stable feelings. As we become increasingly alienated from the realities of our lives we are being drawn to alternative practices to find our inner cosy. Crystals have been proven to be powerful – quartz crystals are used in timepieces for their vibrational properties for a reason. So which crystals can contribute to your cosy corner? Amethyst is known as the all-purpose stone, said to release anxiety and stress. From healing to happiness it's a great all rounder. Rose quartz is said to soothe issues and dilemmas of the heart while jade symbolises tranquillity and purity. Lay them out, pride of place, and give them a polish every now and then.

Cosy listening

What tunes do you find cosy? In my cosiest nana-like state I find Radio 4, or Classic FM is just the ticket. The soothing sound of received pronunciation on the news, homely regional accents on the dramas, and then a bit of classical music, which when listened to on a rainy day, usually peeling root vegetables, makes me feel much more grown up than I am. For some it's the brusque, trumpty 'du-du-du-du-du-du-dum' of *The Archers* and the bucolic narrative washed over us in the background. Van Morrison makes me feel cosy; I associate it with hanging out in my friend Laura's Brighton family kitchen as a teenager. Reggae and Neil Young make me feel good – really good; Soca makes me want to move and dance. Drum and Bass and Garage make me feel nostalgic, rock 'n' roll makes me feel powerful, and a strong, soulful female vocalist makes my heart soar. Anyone who has ever made a mix tape or playlist for another knows how music can express how we are feeling, and the right tracks can amplify our mood or state of mind[7]. Studies show that music has multiple types of direct psychological effects: a regular rhythm helps to regulate breathing and in particular classical music has been proven to help improve heart rate variability, while soothing sounds have been shown to lead to decreased levels of the stress hormone cortisol among strung-out students. A 'cosy Sunday morning' playlist on YouTube has received over 7 million plays in the last year alone, which tells me that people are looking to soundtrack their downtime and the right kind of music can make you feel totally cosy.

A COSY
STATE OF MIND

A cosy state of mind is the greatest medicine. Being sedentary and indulging in self-imposed lethargy, in a 'I'm wedded to this chair' kind of way, is the closest thing to free healing that modern-day society offers us. We are, in this moment, in control of whether we will be turned on, sharp and active – or not. I remember when I was a cub reporter, in my first job, one of my contacts described me as being as 'tenacious as a terrier'. I revelled in it, dined out on that description for years. In fact, recounting that story, along with the name of the person who anointed me this (he was a famous businessman), helped me to get jobs later on in my career. To me, the fact that I wouldn't give up was the greatest accolade. Ploughing on, fighting her corner, striving and winning. What could be better? Achieving a cosy state of mind, that's what.

Unlike hygge, which is beautiful in essence, but too often seen through the lens of interior-design magazines, being cosy is completely personal, affordable and democratic – and it's great for the brain. Voltaire said that illusion is the first of all pleasures, but what comes next? The reality of a real life. Your university joggers and period pants aren't cool enough for Instagram, even with the help of Valencia as a filter, nothing is making your unravelled self seem aspirational to others. So why bother? Being cosy is closer to the solipsistic hug of a hangover, rather than being enlightened. Cosy is your authentic self undone. 'Hygge is like a Disney movie that leaves no place for haemorrhoids . . . It leaves no place for real life,' writes Miska Rantanen in *Päntsdrunk: The Finnish Art of Drinking at Home*.

In cosy, there is no aesthetic to follow; sheepskin rugs and pale floorboards aren't intrinsically connected to our perception of the movement, there is no pressure to be a certain way, or live up to something, but there is one element that should be embraced by all cosy-ites: let's call it *cosy contemplation*. This requires less effort than the ancient art of meditating, and isn't as new age as mindfulness. It's about taking a moment in your cosiness and contemplating where you are, physically and emotionally, and whether or not you like it. Popular mantras, such as, 'Feel the fear and do it anyway,' may have millions of searches online, but try saying, 'I am cosy' out loud and then tune into the immediate surge of warmth it brings. Powerful, eh? Meditation reduces stress, promotes happiness and increases calm. Cosiness does the same thing, with the added anaesthetising layer of a pair of socks (and some jogging bottoms softened through years of wear). Cosiness is as light-hearted as it is profound, and there are precious moments of introspection to be found as you stir milk into your cup of tea, make a simple warming lunch, or stop and listen to the thunder and rain.

Creating an environment conducive to being cosy and switching off is key to your practice (yes, we are calling it that). In the same way that you light candles for a relaxing bath, or charge your crystals for yoga, finding your cosy hotspot is key. Make your own cosy corner – it's vital that it's a corner because enclosed spaces are cosy, open spaces are not – and sit there, on your comfiest chair, and relish the chance to be in your own fug.

Relax every muscle in your body, put your feet up and close your eyes. This may lead to napping, and all the better for it. Slow your roll, take 40 winks, because napping is cosy transcended.

Napping

No longer the preserve of Gramps as he orchestrates the 14.20 at Kempton with the sound of snoring, being good at napping is the new spinning. As the Western world becomes more sleep-deprived, the stigma of sleeping in the day is vanishing and, in its place, a few

right-on brains are encouraging our human instinct to take a load off and enter a short-lived but satisfying coma. Arianna Huffington, the doyenne of mindfulness in the workplace, has installed recharging rooms at her Thrive headquarters in New York so employees can get 40 winks.

Related to an increase in productivity, the art of napping is growing in popularity and it is the backbone of a cosy state of being. We used to boast about being able to function on three hours' sleep – but you only have to spend 24 hours with a child under the age of three to know that sleep is the most precious commodity ever bestowed upon the human race. How much sleep you got last night is the most competitive currency in every single NCT meeting / nursery / lobby / conference room across the land. Me: 'I had 18 minutes' sleep last night in total. Yep, IN TOTAL, and look, I'm still smashing life'. Bored colleague: 'You've got odd shoes on, Laura'.

Talking about sleep is as boring as talking about your dreams, or how 'craaazy' you are after too many negronis, but it's human instinct to share how well you are sleeping, because getting optimum quality shut-eye is the new sign of success. If sleep is a luxury item, then napping is a decadent snack and the ultimate by-product of a wholehearted cosy practice. Winston Churchill, John F. Kennedy, Napoleon and Albert Einstein are all known to have appreciated an afternoon nap, and a study by the Endocrine Society claims that a short nap relieves stress and bolsters the immune system[5].

'My cosiest memory is being a teenager and having a bedroom in my grandparents' house. It was above the boiler so always so toasty and warm. I would stay in bed all day and read magazines: fashion mags that I bought with my waitressing money. These days, cosy is a sofa with quilt and films. There is something about a duvet on the sofa. Blankets are wussy.'

Sharmadean Reid, beauty entrepreneur

Pyjamas and loungewear

Between 2008 and 2015, department store Selfridges saw nightwear grow by 900 per cent, taking the retailer's nightwear business from £200,000 to £2million'.[6] That's a whole lot of jammies. And our love for the comfy life is only increasing, with dressing for bed becoming acceptable as daywear – see posh PJ brands like Olivia von Halle – we love to slouch in style. I have a specific drawer for my cosy clothes, and its contents range from posh PJs to tatty old T-shirts, knackered gymwear, bobbly hiking socks and cashmere jogging bottoms. There's a lot of fleece, a couple of gilets and one particularly well-worn Cos cardi. Dressing to be cosy doesn't always have to mean dressing not to be seen but it's the only time I dress for me: I'm not dressing to impress, or following trends and I don't care who sees me. Off-duty isn't about dressing up as the best version of you, it's about dressing as yourself.

Cosy community

We know that being around people in a genuine, strongly bonded kind of way makes us happier; research carried out by organisations from Harvard to the Institute of Happiness tell us that this is so. It is no wonder, then, that although cosiness can be a solo pursuit, it also works well in the company of friends. But they have to be friends you can lollop and flop with – real, proper mates who you can lie with on the sofa, legs akimbo, with unflinchingly touching arms, touching shoulders, touching feet. Who you can share blankets and eat crisps with. The way you did before you realised you fancied people, that kind of innocent, intimate, sexually benign love you have for your friends love. That is the basis of cosy interactions.

Comrades in cosy should be friends you can share a bar of chocolate with, secure in the knowledge that your non-verbal communications says thank you enough. You need people who make you feel cosy just by being near them. My family friends, the Byford-Winters are such people. I could turn up at their home in Brighton in any state; emotional; inebriated; delighted or otherwise and be welcomed and hugged with something homemade and delicious. It could have been years since my last visit, but there is no judgement, we just assume our positions around the table, or on the sofa, and get cosy. You need pals who you can pull a cracker with, break bread with, share a bottle with. There is no 'I' in cosy but there is a 'co'. It might be a coincidence (no pun intended), but co as in cohabit, company or co-dependent. It helps to be cosy with friends, it fosters a chosen community, even for those of us who have no related family nearby as we move between metropolitan cities, and travel the globe. To have people we can connect with and enjoy the aura of warmth with is important for the soul.

To trust in cosy is to trust in general, and there is a stark difference between connectivity and community. Our social-media snacking encourages us to build a virtual community, which can enrich our lives, but the perpetual pursuit of posting the perfect life can also make us feel pretty crap. Being cosy isn't about being anti-technology but about simplifying life to a position of comfort and (ideally) calm, although I can still feel cosy with a toddler, two cats and a dog clattering around the house.

It may be cheesy, but we all know that a rich, genuine and healthy social life is worth more than money can buy, and we know that to be alone and unsupported is the greatest punishment according to the gospel of cosy (this book). And once we are lucky enough to find our cosy state of being in a safe environment, it encourages us to slow down. And in that slowness we find the space in our minds to examine what it is that is keeping us so busy, and whether we like it very much at all.

COSY OUTDOORS

It's the cyclical nature of walking that makes it such a satisfying thing to do. So says my stepdad Simon, as he steps out of the door to walk his annoying but lovable springer spaniel, Archie, across the South Downs. The crunch of leaves underfoot, the weird way in which we all become friendly again, smiling and saying hello to complete strangers like it's 1967, the headspace and sense of perspective that comes from looking up at big crisp skies.

The liberation of being on a walk, being in the outdoors, which is called great for a reason – is life-affirming, wonderful stuff. The sense of movement and of heading somewhere bestows physical and emotional momentum (and an excuse to find a country pub is always welcome). A country yomp has a beginning, a middle and an end, and when undertaken in the autumn months it requires a cosy outfit and outlook to boot.

Q&A with Liz Nelstrop, walking project officer for the National Trust

What is it about a country walk that makes it feel so cosy in the autumn and winter?
Walking and cosiness tap into innate human needs and experiences. We were designed to walk long distances to find food to gather, cook and socialise around firelight for millennia; walking and warmth are deep within our psyche and souls.

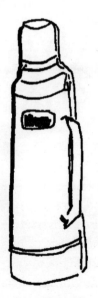

The nights are drawing in and the days are shorter so the end of an afternoon walk is heralded by a much earlier dusk, which also sends us indoors to put on lights and find cosy spaces. The weather is often cold, wet or stormy, so after a walk we feel invigorated and cool, and seek warmth and cosiness in a café, pub or by the fire at home to reset the balance.

Walking also releases physical and mental tension, uses energy and stimulates endorphins, so we are more relaxed and gravitate towards comfortable cosy places to bask in this glow and recuperate.

Why is walking in nature important for our well-being?

Walking on its own is a simple, free and easy way to get active and in doing so can tackle the illnesses of our time (heart, lung, diabetes, obesity) and improve our mental health. But there are a growing number of studies and campaigns showing that a connection with nature amplifies these benefits and increases our health and happiness even further. The rhythmical act of stopping and of absorbing nature: its movement, sounds and colours helps us to process our thoughts. Nature has been found to be uplifting and inspiring and is said to make us more creative and able to solve problems more efficiently. Even city dwellers with only a small green space nearby are more likely to report better mental health outcomes than those without. It can improve vitality, life satisfaction, social connectedness and a sense of meaning in our lives.

Dr Miles Davidson at the University of Derby is a leading researcher into nature connection. His work has identified that if we want to connect people with nature we need to engage them in a way in which they form a relationship with it using the senses, emotion, meaning, compassion and beauty – and when we do, people feel much happier.

Where are some of the cosiest walks in the UK?
The walking opportunities at the National Trust are
endless, both self-led and guided, so it's difficult to
pick just a few. You can blow away the cobwebs by
visiting big landscapes in the Lake District fells, the
Northumbrian coastline or the flowing hills of the
Peak District, or maybe just admire the autumnal
colours of a wander through a beech wood, or stroll
through a landscaped garden as found at Stourhead
or Stowe. Whatever the place, whatever the weather,
getting out into the natural world is always rewarding
– it revitalises our spirits. And then the reward – to
warm up again with steaming hot drinks and a sizzling
fire. What could be better?

My personal favourite would be a family stroll at
Lanhydrock in Cornwall – it has spectacular autumn
colours and not one but two tea rooms to cosy up in
afterwards.

Another lovely walk is the Baggy Point circular on the
North Devon coast where in winter the deep cloud
formations and contrasting light on the sea and cliffs
makes for glorious painterly views. Follow this with
tea at Sandleigh Tea Room, which has a garden,

allotments and Oystercatcher shop with lots of local goodies and you have a perfect cosy walk.

Other cosy autumn and winter walks can be found on p. 159.

'My house in Somerset is the best definition of cosy ... in an eccentric, British way. Everything I have collected from my travels is mixed and matched, and nothing is saved for best. I like it to feel full of colour and light, deeply romantic, timeless, but relaxed and easy. Not in any way contrived. Every time I arrive at home I feel my mood completely change. Somerset feeds my soul. Waking up in the morning, with my bedroom windows flung wide open and nothing but birds to listen to is truly magical. To me, it's about well-being and creating a balance within your own personal space, wherever that may be. Surrounding yourself with great people and family, laughter and love. Good food, great smells and lighting. Our environments make and inspire us.'

**Fashion designer Alice Temperley
on her personal cosy**

Camping

'Are you holding on? We're about to take a corner! Wooooaaaaahhhh', said my mum, behind the enormous steering wheel of our bright red, VW campervan in 1991. The sliding side door had come off its hinges some time ago, and had to be held on by a willing passenger (me) while in transition. Cue us racing down Halstow hill in Greenwich, and pulling up outside my school with me gripping onto the sliding door for dear life. The shame? It was character building. At the time I wish we'd had a Volvo like the other parents, but on reflection that campervan was my safe, cosy space. In the winter months it sat on our driveway and I used it as a club house for me and my neighbourhood friends. In the summer months we packed it up for camping trips, setting off in the dead of night to Dover, to catch the ferry under the stars and arriving in France in time for breakfast. A portable version of our family home, the camper was supremely cosy. There were duvets, cushions and camping snacks, all of my books and toys came with us, and we sat reading, or playing cards inside the van, parked up in a French farm field when the temperature dropped outside.

Everyone was happy in the camper, we were quite literally, happy campers. My parents were on their holidays and loved the freedom of living on the road, my sister was a toddler so being able to run around a campsite for hours on end was pure bliss. For me, being in nature, and in a new setting every few days gave me an exciting anonymity, I had dozens of pen pals and learnt to wash up dishes in a camping wash block. The van was always a bit rusty, but she never felt past it, carrying us to and between some of the best memories of my life. I cried when we sold it, and I still well up when I think of her now.

Caravans, bell tents, cabins and bog-standard four-man jobbies . . . Camping is a cosy pursuit and it's an activity that's booming. A rise in domestic tourism has been charted since the vote for Brexit was announced, with the data suggesting it's cost-related as savvy consumers look to spend less on recreation.

The Cool Camping website reported a 50 per cent rise in glamping bookings over the first three months of 2018, compared with the same period of 2017. I believe all roads lead back to cosy. Domestic and global politics are making many of us feel uncertain, anxious even, and staying close to home is a sensible response.

More than 17 million camping and caravanning trips were taken by UK adults in 2016, according to Mintel, and this is expected to rise by almost another million this year. And it just so happens that there is little more cosy a feeling than the one you get from lying in a tent as the rain patters down outside and the petrichor lingers, especially at the end of summer. Could it be something to do with the size of the tent, which is always small, or just big enough for you and your companions? There is no surplus, nowhere to get lost. On the scale of cosy, an unwieldy, rambling country pile scores lower than a barge on the Norfolk Broads. A temporary nest, these spaces are manageable, simple and sweet. My mum, Lynne, an infant school headteacher, describes her job as the 'cosiest in the world', the small realm of the classroom so cosy, so safe. It's made so by the collective energy of the children and their teacher, who forge the environment together. It's a little community in just a few hundred square feet.

COSY STAYS

St Monans, Fife: a coastal village on the east coast of
Scotland with a population of about 1500, otherwise
known as the coldest, wettest place on planet earth. It's
the year 1990, and on top of a steep cliff in there stands
a caravan. The North Sea winds batter its corrugated
aluminium exterior and rain hammers its lightweight
door. Inside, is eight-year-old me in a lime-green shell
suit sat with my granny playing cards and eating
biscuits. I went to granny's caravan for a week every
year and it felt like months – months of pure heaven.

I have always been drawn to a small singular world.
Whether it's at a cottage in Wales or in a house in the
New Forest, visiting friends or relatives, living someone else's life for a short spell has always appealed to
me. The basic daily routine of going to get milk from
the local shop or to a new pub in the evening, doing
usual things in an unusual world, is comforting to me.

Today I go to cosy places for holidays, preferring the
Mendips to the Maldives, I like the British Isles and the
ease of travelling there. My holidays are mainly about

de-stressing, so the less time spent at Stansted Airport, the better. When I do arrive home I spend weeks working out how I too could live in a yurt in the middle of Devon. And I search for the answer in the most seriously deluded way. I have been known to engage estate agents, to visit properties to try and find my dream cosy retreat. However, until life finds a way of offering me the means to be able to afford the cottage (or caravan) of my dreams, cosy stays will have to do; here are my favourite few:

The Pig, near Bath
(and other locations in the South West)
thepighotel.com
You'll find the cosiest stay in the UK tucked into the folds of the Mendip Hills. The setting here might be

a grand country house, but the feeling inside The Pig is one of intimate familiarity, strengthened by the abundance of creature comforts, from the slabs of cake on arrival to the kitchen-garden fare and locally sourced fizz on the menu. And it's an absolute joy to be inside the potting-shed massage hut, having a rubdown, while it rains.

Shore Cottage at Carskiey, Mull of Kintyre, Scotland

carskiey.com

Silence, solitude and spectacular scenery are the order of the day at this remote cottage tucked away at the edge of a rambling Scottish estate, mere steps away from the Irish Sea. The fireplace and resident board games are crucial companions, as are the seals that dance outside your window in the slate-grey waters.

Dolphin Cottage, Ceredigion, Wales, Y Cartws

dolphinbay.co.uk

Unlikely and tiny, this one-bedroom cottage is at the end of a winding, forest-flanked road in Wales, and at the bottom of someone's garden. It's an affordable, rustic and well-located cosy place that's big enough for two, and close to the beach for fish and chips and big choppy waves. I'd move in here if I could.

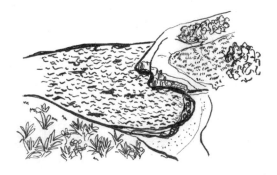

COSY FILMS

It's raining outside, giving you permission to watch a feel-good film and do little else. These are my choices for indulging in cinematic cosiness.

Little Women
The big winter scenes of love and the sisterhood in this nineties classic will make you feel warm and happy.

The Holiday
For the cute cottage, the smoking chimney and Cameron Diaz's cosy wardrobe.

When Harry Met Sally
With its iconic scenes of walking through Central Park, it's the ultimate cosy romcom.

Any of the Harry Potter films
Snowy themes and season changes abound, plus there are the endless messages of comfort, love and support.

Mary Poppins
A nostalgic, cosy vision of old London.

The Snowman
The introduction by David Bowie is more soothing than hot chocolate.

It's a Wonderful Life
A devastating story, but synonymous with Christmas.

You've Got Mail
'Don't you love New York in the fall?' Also see *When Harry Met Sally*.

Dead Poets Society
All that corduroy, those jumpers and the fallen leaves.

COSY READS

There are two types of people on this earth: those who read voraciously because they live for books – the arc of a great narrative, learning, brushing up on vocab, escaping into the pages of a story. And then there are those who can take or leave a good tale. I'm a reader with an average appetite. There are colleagues of mine who devour two books a week; I, however, clear about seven a year. I might do one on a summer holiday, another in the lead-up to Christmas and potentially another one to restart my mind in January. Then the rest of the year is made up of Instagram recommendations and books with nice covers that I see and read on the commute. There are some books, however, that will stay with me for a lifetime, the ones I read as a teen – more often than not, they still work well on a Sunday afternoon in front of the fire.

The Six Bullerby Children by **Astrid Lindgren**
Nothing comforts like re-reading a childhood favourite, and the book that cossets and soothes me like no other is *The Six Bullerby Children*, a lesser-known work by *Pippi Longstocking* author, Astrid Lindgren.

Carrot-topped Pippi might have grabbed all the attention, but this sweet book about the domestic adventures of children in a three-farm village in rural Sweden deserves lots of love. Nothing terribly wild happens – one chapter involves a lost tooth, another a snow storm – but it's wholesome, charming and as healing as a strong cup of sugary tea.

The Cazalet Chronicles by Elizabeth Jane Howard

This series follows the fortunes of the sprawling and eccentric Cazalet family, beginning in 1937 with *The Light Years*. Howard narrates the seemingly ordinary events of family life – both in London and at their Sussex country pile – with fascinating period detail. Thankfully, there are five volumes to see you through a dark winter. It's the ultimate in comfort reading.

Love, Nina by Nina Stibbe

The hugely entertaining collection of Stibbe's letters to her sister Victoria during a five-year period when she lived and worked as a nanny to Mary-Kay Wilmers, the editor of the *London Review of Books*. Living at Wilmers's home in Gloucester Crescent, London NW1, Stibbe unexpectedly found herself in the heart of literary north London. She writes with great affection for the characters she encounters, which include Alan Bennett, who makes several hilarious cameos and turns out to be a dab hand at fixing dodgy appliances. Funny and genuinely heart-warming.

On Beauty by Zadie Smith

There's nothing better than getting lost in an epic family saga when the elements are raging outside and this powerful, ambitious novel is one of the very best of the genre. Echoing EM Forster's *Howards End*, it covers large, expansive issues of marriage, friendship and clashing cultures while also weaving in beautiful observations on weather, city life and yes, beauty. Gloriously witty and perceptive, this is one to hibernate with.

Circle of Friends by Maeve Binchy

A classic coming-of-age tale, *Circle of Friends* follows good-natured Benny and her best friend Eve as they go from a sleepy town in Ireland to university in Dublin and encounter selfish Nan, handsome Jack and endless romance and heartbreak. Like all of Binchy's books, it radiates warmth and wisdom. One for a gloomy autumn afternoon.

Season Songs by **Ted Hughes**

Season Songs was originally aimed at children but, as Hughes himself said, the poems 'grew up' as he wrote them. The Winter poems are evocative, complex, beautiful and transcendent all at once, the centrepiece being 'Snow and Snow', which showcases Hughes's transformative imagination. Words to savour when the nights draw in.

Persuasion by **Jane Austen**

All of Austen's classics could have made the cosy cut, but for me, the clear winner is *Persuasion*. Anne Elliot is my ultimate Austen heroine – sympathetic, practical and intelligent. Hibernate with a cup of tea and swoon over sensitive and smart Captain Wentworth. This is a book filled with hope, and its portrayal of love persisting and conquering all warms the heart. Simply superb.

Little Women by **Louisa May Alcott**

' "Christmas won't be Christmas without any presents," grumbled Jo, lying on the rug.' This opening line sets the scene for the beloved tale of the March sisters growing up in a quiet New England town. Each time I return to this grade-A classic it reveals something I hadn't noticed before.

Bridget Jones's Diary by **Helen Fielding**

Nothing could be more cosy than finding comfort in familiar characters you know inside out. I'm certain to die having never read Proust but regularly revisit this and find myself muttering, 'Oh, come along, Bridget,' at least twice a day. Can we even remember a time before emotional fuckwits and smug marrieds? This perfect novel made me screech with laughter when I first devoured it as a teenager and still does to this day.

How to Eat by **Nigella Lawson**

Yes, this is technically a cookbook, but in Nigella's hands it's so much more, and I return to this classic constantly for its exquisitely soothing words as much as for its delicious recipes. Nigella's love for both cooking and eating can be found on every dog-eared, splattered page. Homely and life-affirming, it appears

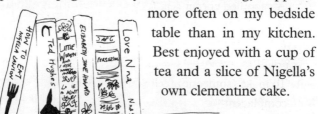

more often on my bedside table than in my kitchen. Best enjoyed with a cup of tea and a slice of Nigella's own clementine cake.

Compiled by Niamh O'Keeffe.

Cosy kəʊzi/

adjective
1. Giving a feeling of comfort, warmth and relaxation.
2. 'The flickering lamp gave the room a cosy, lived-in air.'

noun
1. A soft covering to keep a teapot, boiled egg, etc. hot.
2. 'A photograph of Smith pouring tea from a pot with a knitted cosy.'
3. BRITISH
   A canopied corner seat for two.

verb
informal
1. To make (someone) feel comfortable or complacent.
2. 'She cosied him and made out she found him irresistible.'

CHRISTMAS

'My idea of Christmas, whether old-fashioned or modern, is very simple: loving others. Come to think of it, why do we have to wait for Christmas to do that?'

Bob Hope

Christmas is the time of year, and really the only time of year, when I notice other people's shoulders visibly relaxing and their hostilities softening. Whether on the London Underground or walking past one another on the street as the big day closes in, our hearts open up. Of course, some people hate Christmas, and many don't celebrate it, but I love it. It is without a doubt, my favourite time of the year. It was in mid-December in a sandwich shop near Trafalgar Square when I found myself wallet-less while trying to buy a turkey sandwich, and a generous customer in the queue stepped in and bought it for me. Would this have happened in the month of June? I don't know – but I do know we're not supposed to be grinchy at Christmas, and that being a living breathing humbug is not a good look. So come winter, we should dial up the niceness and give being friendly a go. It lasts about a month, or actually until the early hours of New Year's Day, when the sound of people having too much fun in the street outside your bedroom window grinds your 'new year, new me' gears. On balance, the end of December, in the deep mid-winter, feels like a time more for loving and giving than any other in the calendar, and good vibes plus cold weather equal supremely cosy times.

The unifying quality of this time of year is something to behold. It's not the smell of Norwegian spruce (if you do a real tree), mulled everything and a turkey (or nut roast) crisping in the oven that folds warm, fuzzy feelings into our brains, but the collective cosy sense of everyone going through the same thing that does it. Many of us are scheduling guilt visits to neglected relatives and embarking on far-from-relaxing trips to buy gifts that we desperately want people to love, and come Christmas Eve, we are trying to leave work early and not be standing on the train after 5pm. We are in this together. That, and shopping for a tree, digging out the knackered decorations and the predictability of untangling the lights, these moments are mostly lovely, as is the debate about trying something new for Christmas lunch this year, and then settling on turkey for the 12,486th year in a row.

Atheist, Christian, Muslim or Jewish: the essence of winter – togetherness and warmth – are common themes for us all to enjoy. Of course, when it comes to the best Christmas gift of all (for someone who is lucky enough to have a healthy social life): it's an excuse to become utterly isolated. No one will email you on Christmas Day, no one will try to sell you windows or encourage you to embark on a 'no win, no fee' lawsuit. No one will interfere with your ultimate cosy downtime. There is no 'Sorry to bother you' on Christmas Day, and being 'too busy' to meet up is an acceptable excuse and, joy of joys, the news cycle vanishes into thin air for three whole days. There are no breaking headlines (what a downer that would be), there's no fake news, there are no politics, unless they come in meme form or as jokes fired across the Christmas lunch table, and we have no idea what is happening in the world, other than the fact it is still turning and your living room, complete with its comfort and joy, is rotating away on top of it.

The most hectic thing that happens is the preparation of Christmas lunch. The walls of the kitchen shine with condensation and the trifle cools on top of the fridge because no surface is clear and it's too cold to open the windows; people smoke just inside the back door – rules don't apply. Everyone is busy and everyone has a job: chop this, wash that, boil this, wrap that. And really, compared with our daily lives, this is how busy we should feel – it's temporary and rewarding, and it's enchanting.

Although Christmas provides us with a landscape to disconnect from the world around us as we hibernate temporarily, it does force us to connect with our kin. At what other time of year do we find ourselves in a room with so many people that we share DNA with (the sexual-health clinic and funerals notwithstanding)? And despite the fact making small talk while clad in something red, green and polyester isn't the most fun, the connection is invaluable, even if it's to decide that you feel far cosier and more comfortable with your chosen family back home in Sheffield, rather than the one you were born into in Glasgow.

Juggling the simple pleasures in navigating family life at Christmas is a metaphor for as demanding as daily life should get – well, that's my theory anyway. It's not easy but it's not unpleasant (not always) and it's manageable and well rehearsed. There's no severe anxiety, or rather, there shouldn't be. There are none of the things that plague our modern lives; the stress catalysts of unpredictable work, and unbearable pressure vanish even just for a brief moment, and whether or not the turkey is done is the only thing that matters now.

> 'The winter brought the heaviest snow I'd ever seen.
> The snow fell steadily all through the night. When I
> woke up, the room was filled with light and silence,
> and I knew then it was to be a magical day.'
> **Older James, *The Snowman***

Christmas is the only time of year that cosiness is allowed to eclipse chaos, and we should embrace it with gusto. We are allowed to reconnect with ourselves. More than New Year, Christmas is a time for recalibrating states of mind, friendships, work and life choices, and beyond. When are you at your most brilliantly basic? When you're on the sofa at your nan's house. Reflecting on your life there, as your aunt passes the fags round and your uncle mixes glasses of sherbert yellow snowballs, it's here that you'll find a mindful moment. Rather than being one of the 3 million people commuting for 4 hours a day, your sharp elbows bend inwards at home, or at least they should. Being with your family or your chosen loved ones is a true leveller and helps solidify the idea that (cliché incoming) being happy is all that matters. These are the people who don't care how many Instagram likes your last post got, and that's good for all of us once in a while because before you know it, you'll be 78 years old and worrying about the pipes freezing, too.

The bit in-between

And then comes the in-between bit, the bit I adore. In Norway they call it *Romjul* (and they really know how to do cosy in Norway), some call it Twixtmas, but I prefer The Christmas Perineum, or Food Week. Whatever you call it, if Christmas takes the edge off daily life, then the bit between Christmas and New Year obliterates the boundaries completely. Those days just sit there doing nothing and are infinitely less challenging than an episode of *Love Island*. By this stage, in fact, no one even knows their own name or what day it is, my brain now resembles an unwrapped Ferrero Rocher, as expendable as that wafer cannonball beneath the chocolate and for some beloved reason, it's completely acceptable to remain in your pyjamas for most, or all, of No Man's Week, if that's what you desire. No one requires anything of you, and you require nothing of anyone else. You have almost ceased to exist and it's marvellous. It is your duty to be cosy, you are obliged to tuck in.

'Cosy for me is the new mindfulness, it's not as trendy as the commercial interpretation of hygge might have been perceived; it's what families across the UK do on a daily basis. It's the things that bind this country together – cups of tea, toast and sitting in front of the fire whether that's log or electric. I suppose getting cosy has always been a key cornerstone of my life without me even acknowledging it before now.'

Henry Holland, designer and TV personality

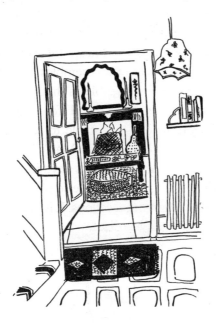

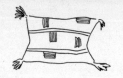

A FINAL NOTE

So there you have it; that was your journey through the soothing balm that is cosy living. You've made it to the end and just as there is a sense of satisfaction in finishing a book, I guarantee you that double such contentment lies in wait under the nearest blanket, on the closest sofa and at the bottom of a hot cuppa.

I hope this book has filled you with ideas of little ways you can cosify your life and that you spread the warmth and comfort that comes from feeling cosy to others.

REFERENCES

1 www.dezeen.com/2014/10/28/measuring-the-craft-economy-3-billion-pounds-uk-crafts-council/, accessed 16 September 2018

2 https://www.telegraph.co.uk/science/2018/03/11/knitting-should-prescribed-nhs-lower-blood-pressure-reduce-depression/, accessed 16 September 2018

3 https://www.businessinsider.com/here-are-15-ridiculous -celebrity-backstage-demands-2012-4?IR=T

4 https://www.health.harvard.edu/staying-healthy/blue-light -has-a-dark-side

5 www.sciencedaily.com/releases/2015/02/150210141734.htm, accessed 16 September 2018

6 www.standard.co.uk/fashion/trends/while-you-were-sleeping-we-chart-the-rise-of-our-relationship-with-pyjamas-a3213331.html, accessed 16 September 2018

7 www.ncbi.nlm.nih.gov/pubmed/15813154, accessed 16 September 2018

Cosy walks

- www.nationaltrust.org.uk/lists/cosy-tea-rooms-and-cafs
- www.nationaltrust.org.uk/lists/walks-with-cosy-cafes
- www.nationaltrust.org.uk/lists/our-best-winter-walks
- www.nationaltrust.org.uk/lists/coastal-walks-with-cafes

ACKNOWLEDGEMENTS

There are two fantasies that I have been known to act out in my head before I drift to sleep. One is being at a wedding. The singer hasn't turned up and there is chaos, heartbreak everywhere. I step in on stage and save the day with my incredible rendition of 'At Last'. I sing my best version to astonished friends, there are blown minds all over the marquee, they have known me for years 'but never knew I was so vocally gifted'. The second fantasy is this, writing a page of acknowledgements in my hugely clever, successful, serialised, translated into a million languages, book. I then read it out at my book launch, a bit like when Bridget Jones introduces Mr Titspervert at the launch of Kafka's motorbike but with more style. Who to thank for the book of *Cosy*? Well without my family, the people who have been responsible for paying the heating bill for half of my life, I wouldn't know what cosy was. So thank you to all of them – my mum has already got the bumper dedication, but she is quite literally the cosiest woman I know, being in her presence makes me feel warmer, and she's never out of Uggs. My sister Jess who is equally as cosy as me and has a serious penchant for a PJ and a packet of biscuits, Dario and Alida, my dad Phil who is Scottish, and as a result being cold and loving it is in my genes

– and he and my mum gave me some of my cosiest childhood memories – if he hadn't ever taken me sledging and given me soup in front of the fire to warm up I would have no concept of what it is to be cosy. My step-dad Simon who helped me with the structure for the book and inspired the cosy outdoors chapter and who has always been my champion, and of course my daughter Astrid. Being a mum is the ultimate cosy feeling, never is a time more tucked in than those early weeks with your new babe, so thank you darling, clever, funny daughter for choosing me to be your mummy, and for the cosy times I share with you. My nan, who taught me the art of cosy cooking, and my gramps whose big cosy cuddles are something I wish I could bottle. Can I acknowledge my cat Iggy? No, too far. Too weird.

There is one person in my life who is actually my right arm, and that is Niamh O'Keeffe, she wrote a few words for this book (because she is hugely talented) and she is generous, and kind and I couldn't be more grateful for the support she gives me on a daily basis. Thank you. The sensational Dolly Alderton for allowing me to badger you into submission for your fab note on cosy and to the beautiful and bright, Sophie Dahl, for your kind words. Huge gratitude to the brilliant Lauren Whelan who is my publisher at Yellow Kite and came up with this idea in the first place, to Liz Gough for believing in the power of cosy and to the gifted Imogen Fortes who saved me from myself, edited out the clangers and gave me some great advice. Thank you to my agent Charlie for your support. A huge thank you to the sensational Rose Electra Harris. Rose drew the beautiful, charming, funny illustrations for the book of *Cosy*. She took the project on at a moment's notice and was a complete trooper. Thank you for being so patient and for actualising the vision for the cosy scenes I had in my mind's eye. The illustrations bring this book to life and that's all down to you. Thank you Sarah Christie for being patient with my revisions and I absolutely love the cover (after our 76435th version). Thank you Anna Van Praagh for taking the time to read an early proof, I trust you implicitly and took on every one of your edits. Jeremy Lee you were the first person I asked to contribute to the book and you said yes with such gusto it gave me a much-needed burst of confidence. Melissa Hemsley you are such a wonderful champion, Jo Ellison thank you for making the book sound cleverer, Bay Garnett and Christopher Kane, I adore you in the most true and non-fashion way. Alice Temperley you are a cosy queen, thank you to Lorraine Acornley, Liz Nelstrop, Jade Harwood and Sharmadean Reid, to Virginia Norris for the PR advice and to Paul, for always being kind. To my friend Rowan Erlam for being you and, thank you to Henry Holland for, as always, letting me put words into your mouth.